Carry On
(Elegies)

Adam Deutsch

Carry On (Elegies)
2nd Edition

Copyright © 2014-2018 / Adam Deutsch
978-1-943899-06-7

Some poems in this collection appeared in some wonderful journals, sometimes in different versions:
"In Ithaca Once" —*Arsenic Lobster*
"Pre-War" & "The Center for Personal Growth is Next Door to Cremation Services" —*InDigest*
"Descriptor" — *Prick of the Spindle*
"Off Hours" —*Similar Peaks*
"Packing Heat"—*Thrush Poetry Journal*
"Deleting Dead People from the Address Book"
        —*White Stag*
"Migrations and Monuments" has an epigraph from a full work that was once at www.ngs.noaa.gov/INFO/fourcorners.shtml

Cover: A photo of an MGB's fender

Glovebox Poems is a chap/zine project.
More is at AdamDeutsch.com

Contents

The Roads Will Be Closed   5
Packing Heat   6
What Cuts through the Woods   8
The Droplight Is a Sun   9
Hibernators   10
Kinda like It's the Sabbath   11
Migrations & Monuments   12
Devastation   14
Great Aunt, Winter, & Sun   15
The Center for Personal Growth Is Next
       Door to Cremation Services   16
Strangers, Autumn, & Gray   18
Pre-War   19
Carry On   20
Descriptor   22
Our Advances Are Not Unique   24
Pingueculum or Pterygium   25
Us This Day   26
Artisans   28
Containable Noise   29
No Way to Live   30
Dryer   32
In Ithaca Once   33
Golden Hill   34
Deleting Dead People from the Address Book   36
Returning   37

The Roads Will Be Closed

If everyone keeps their brights on,
there: a beauty is stretched out
that we just have to leave be.

A kid plays air drums
in first period algebra
with unsharpened pencils.
There is no incident
to report down to the office.
He harms nothing.
His lunch is in a sack
in his bag, with or without
a note from his mother.

I was schooled, too,
and my parents,
their sisters and brothers,
looking at the bomb shelter signs
beside the basement doors.
All of our eyes opened
in anticipation of the blast,
a pause,
the hot sweep, and aftermath.

Packing Heat

Lockheed rings, that vehicle inspector job
I look good for. Human
Resources has a bank of vital questions.

A show of sturdy thew: I'm out of the bed.
Which caliber rounds could be among
pocket cough drop wrappers, crumpled
receipts, coin? What discovered contraband.

I'm comfortable with rotating shifts,
have no arrests, and can submit
to random testings. I must wrestle down
genuine objection to wearing a gun.

These answers are what they need, along
with my motivation: What do I want
from a company to give all I've got,
to draw and squeeze in the clutch?

Shelter. Compassion in semi-weekly
visits to a market for produce. Our fill.
I haven't worked in almost an entire
year, and can bear a uniform's weight.

I only claim I am the man for this level
of clearance, wear no shoes on the porch,
hang up and stand through sunset unarmed.

What Cuts through the Woods

Those orange signs show up on trees
and only make things worse.

Neighboring ranch hands and land
tenders, raw from a city council dispute,

dump a pack of wild turkeys
at the foot of my aunt's quarter mile

driveway. They bobble and charge
the abandoned railroad bed. She says

dogs and deer will take them down
through the next two or three nights.

That smoke on the wind from a neighbor
property was a local wood

holding oxygen unpocketed in low pops.
We all drink from the same well.

The Droplight Is a Sun

What you see by, in an hour you sip the nightstand
water. It tans your face while you pull an engine,
quick like a young tooth, from gooied mounts,
push excess dabs of that heat into stain worn jeans
hung on garage hooks, an undomesticated hide.

Radiate, even tucked in behind the latched doors,
under the down and multiple threads.
Even when the day isn't clear, someone
certainly takes care: the maintenance of you.

Deep rest repairs the body for daily wear:
warmed walls in socket wrenches pressed
to the six sides of each bolt
that holds so much vehicle together,
lock-washered tight by the hands of those
living in the hours where we do not.

Hibernators

It's another story of collapse:
just look to a flock of pigeons
in an acute dive toward
under the bench for bread,
sure as the path
is worn through woods
going thataway.

The ceiling is missing
a couple of tiles. We wait
for daylight to dig
through the universe above
the basement.
Patient, spread out
to the tune of deep
ignition in the belly
of a gas burner in the corner
with grasshoppers who've never
been outside the concrete,
sheet rock, and beams.

Call them frog bugs, creeping,
harmless. They live here, too.

Kinda like It's the Sabbath

When I rise anytime after six,
it's in panic. Entire seconds
spun frantic, lost in the blazing sense
that I'm running late and will be behind
for the rest of my life, letting you down.

A clutch slave cylinder is busted,
leaks viscous fluid in my hoodie's pouch.
There'll be no driving today, kinda like
it's the Sabbath. Twisted tears of newspaper
plug the holes and soak. I can walk
the weight of this bleeding part.

A woman, mom—not mine, but someone's,
maybe yours—walks a giant white Labrador
nosing at my lazy grip. I learn he's twelve
years old, just had a five pound tumor removed
from his shaved side, is acting spanking new:
a rubber ball hatched from a plastic egg,
tossed on the kitchen tile.

Migrations & Monuments

"Regardless of the technical nuances, we can confidently say that, considering the relatively primitive surveying technology of the day, the remote and difficult prevailing field conditions, and uncertainty in the survey's beginning coordinates for Ship Rock, Chandler Robbins' survey was a resounding success…Finally, we cannot overemphasize the fact that the aforementioned technical geodetic details are absolutely moot when considering any question of the correctness or validity…the location of the physical monument is the ultimate authority in delineating a boundary."
— William Stone,
"Where Exactly is Four Corners," 5/15/09

Expecting mothers living near
a particle accelerator
have to inform the engineers
of the main facility.
Whatever happens beyond
that, far as we know, is mystery.

In accordance with the lease,
permission is mandatory to drill
and wedge a peep hole in our front door.

Your rucksack is washed. It hangs
in the shower—the small pocket
full of hotel shampoos
have leaked their goo.
They drown under the spigot,
spumed to excess, and all

the where-have-you-beens
are rinsed and drained.

If you are able to gather
enough of the skin
that cushions your spine,
you can make holes
large enough for rings

to become suspended
from the ceiling,
provided studs
are up there
and strong.

Devastation

The man on the door has lost two friends
in these last seven days. Suicides.
Thorn rose tattoos, thin vines, spreading the pitch
of bare torso. A full stein in sharp pieces.

We've tried to explain: Just because
there's a break in the road-side iron rails
doesn't mean a route's been cut to follow.

My dentist climbs the chair's side
for the pull, fissures a deep line. In my jaw
under the gum, through bone,
I feel your weather an hour before
the squall hammers on your nest.

I hear thunder, and it stops
my heart to kill, even the lights.

Great Aunt, Winter, & Sun
for Marilyn Adler

Each of us lifts a full shovel
and sends the earth down,
stabbing the tool
deep in a mound. The rite
is that we're to bury
our own dead and hear
the hollow low thud on the box
at the bottom. Mostly echo.

She was a small woman,
frail woven, sharp-angled.
Everyone drops their scoop—
cousin Frank forgets, is too moved,
must eliminate the void
until a sweat brings him back.
Still, the *we* never really fill
the hole. There are men
paid just for that, who pull
levers on a machine,
doze with louder cries
and bigger teeth
than most blood can harbor.

The Center for Personal Growth Is Next Door to Cremation Services

Tim brings his wife
to the courtyard
in a stainless steel egg,
reckoning she
could use the air.

I've got one—
a dash of friend
in a small vase,
and Murphy's got one too,
sets out a bronze cube
bearing a sunken cross.
He stores it away
near canned greens
in a desk fan box.
His old partner.
A business associate.
An old dog. A doc.

We're of a people
who keep absence
near. Handy
as duct tape.

The ground
is for a different kind,
with fierce ideas
on remaining whole.

Strangers, Autumn, & Gray
for those in the City of Ithaca Cemetary

A whole other mass, back in their ground,
slowly pushes, worms the pipes,
and gravels our foundations.

I ride a bus that weaves gradually up
the west side of the hill, and hold back
somersaulting down in return home
through the green. I'd surely blunt
on each of the stones, a flailing avalanche
on deep chiseled markers at the top,
and come a cropper way down, the monuments
abraded smooth, generations'
worth of runoff, drizzle, and pour.

Pre-War

Bicycles stacked in this basement add
up to either eighty dollars in scrap
or a monkey bar obstacle course
to the damn water main, frozen again.

We thrash down lumber steps
for lessons on how to sweep, monkish
below clouds, shingle, gutter weaving
maple saplings, porous stone,
locust-shells-in-waiting dirt.

There is life within single panes, sitting up
in the front room colored like carnage in a
barn.
Peace seeps like wind through window seals
that kept our tiny world mostly dry.

Noise carries through dusted rooms,
that simple grace of a plane holding on,
then letting go of Fat Man and Little Boy.

Carry On
for DJ Robinson

Can ashes be brought onboard,
or must we check them
with the larger cargo?
Could I set this miniature vessel
on the same surface where food
is served in the light's brilliant fade and lull?

Through the window is a canyon
he could have loved,
all that absence of rooves,
where one razors loose a dozen leashes
lashed around a self's own wrists.
There's a basset hound at each end
tugging away, or mauling the ground.
We are never alone in any event.
My brother who slipped

inks deep under young dermal layers,
sat in prisons nearby borders.
We were cornered by the window in a diner booth
out on the island, and became older
sailing in a sedan with a pony in the back seat.

We're exiles of an old country's
long gone century, erased analog tape.

We're plowing through this life
in our longings so mighty, a bird swoops
up ahead and is creamed by the bumper.

Descriptor

for Xavier Robinson

These are fingers that cannot
feel ink on the book's page,
pressed, but they run the hills
and sloped lines of other skin.

Blood lifts these lines. A geyser-
like pressure presses hard
then calms under fleshed ceilings:
swell from a whole night's rest.
So many visions are sewn in
to trundling, beating beauty.

Your father's was not an art
of tragedy that comes from, say,
the fired gun. Nor were their scars
from glowing cloth-hanger wire.

These shapes were tucked under,
into us, with a *machine*. It made
compassionate ligatures from small pokes,
more curious sensations
than burning kinds of pain. Each one

a young child, exploding to share,
pulling at your cuff. Come here.
Come and take a look. Lookie
what I made. You've got to see this.

Our Advances Are Not Unique

A sugar maple's arms built a chest
around the block's telephone wires, and roots
tore up a few slabs we shared in the walk.

The town razed all the trees to chips over
that one winter, but left what they created—
a timber holding on to important calls
up there, where two birds, at least, dwell.

We stood below their home and rubbed
oils made from our palms on the toes
of high-laced oxblood leather boots.

Poured fresh, a concrete path
between the street gutter, garden and yard,
the living pass under where others live.

Pingueculum or Pterygium

Whatever.

They can fold a flap
on my eye's face
and hit it
with a laser.

It's safe.
They do it
all the time
to everyone.

Unless you're
some kind
of kung fu
fighter, it'll
hold.

Us This Day

Canners beat
the recycling trucks
to our curb.

Deer've nibbled
the neighbor peach tree,
while a man keeps his vow
to never wear white
shoes again.

He wanders out
for a loaf of bread
he'll slice as he pleases.

This world won't flinch
at the groggy,
their stretching from dreams
and gatherings.

And a girl who sees it all
and hears,
in every car tire's turn,
the name of a saint.

She recalls, from a collective
memory of ether,
great fastings commonly mistaken
as sacrifice of sanity.

It's committed devotion,
a full majestic dish.
Our hunger is buried
in a shadeless field
where we muster,
just about daily,
spread on our backs.

Artisans

Waves get distilled in a foam,
applied to our wounds.

A machine we shall never think of as a gun,
intends to ornament up these bodies
we carry some simple life around in.

A new badge covers over
decades of sun weathering and raunch.

Elsewhere, a woman in neon hair
wears baby brass knuckles
around her neck. The stencils she's cut:
some are etched out sheets of tin or aluminum.

Others are sliced from pizza box lids
so they'll die after only a few sprays,
soaked and withered under creation's gentle coat.

Containable Noise

I've awoken
in spinning cars
interested
in specifically where
we were, and, obligated, screamed
into stretched ragtop
skin rooves.

Only sometimes
do those sounds make sense.
If these were the last of them,
what I meant was
I didn't mean
for any of us
to join the stream.

No Way to Live

This one show had everyone crapulous,
all hidden remorse in flashy frames.
In another episode, everyone's
accused of murder, or else they're
getting killed, or beside a pool
cooking in the sun without waking.

This is reporting. A young man's throat
closed in the hospital's lobby. The nurse
said he was blue before his knees
came to rest on the tile. After, the ashes
arrived, sealed in a small jar and
just like that
there's too much stuff in my place
to consider moving.

Once upon a time, a salad plate
slid in front of me, and I'd talk
down to the cherry tomatoes,
taunt them like small prisoners
at the prongs of the fork.

I hope they can forgive.

Like you, they've become a part of me,
teeth beasting down
on themselves, especially in nights
with thirst, when nobody else
needs to get further hunted.

Dryer

A bartender decides
a dollar no longer equals
4 quarters, gives 3 for the felt.

He's out of touch with his craft.
Pours and pulls but can't finesse
that soda gun
to only drizzle
the raw syrup.

The laundry mat is 24 hours,
the night shift covered
by a machine gun turret.
Drop extra coin for
the 20 more minutes
those shirts always need.

Pinch the jeans
in the rolled up
back window,
and floor it home.

In Ithaca Once

I left her, barely alive
up in the rental, studying
our physics above a garage.
A BMW sidecar was flipped over
next to that loyal desk I stole
from a university department.

That landlord had his tea, found
a notebook in the top drawer,
called collect, mailed it out
beyond cascade confine.

All of those tight rope bridges
daring city planning officials
pulled across the gorges
had nothing to do with it.
We just froze like smelt.

And then, that one pizza place
with free delivery through midnight
locked up, the three ovens
all vanished in morning.

Golden Hill

Don't pay any attention
to how many bumpers
have kissed you.

The market's T is red neon
like it's trying to grow
into a mission's cross head.

Behind all those furious
sunned succulents
a retired woman who's kept
long hair fires up a wet saw
and slices at subway tile.

There are a few nights
the rain will never stop
pulling warmth through
all the walls.

I have to run to the store.
I have to pull a scarf tight.

Every beet I cut
looks like a heart
on fire in a Mexican
art piece.

Oh, Adam—sliver light said—
if you were a real man
you'd cut your own hair
with a sharpened stick.

Out there is a flower dealer
watching a woodpecker
with priorities in order.

This is who you've been
constant with grace and time.
Upkept and polished
to gaze upon day after year.

Deleting Dead People from the Address Book

This is the conversation we repeat,
our washings-away.

Were I a bit older I'd be scratching at their houses,
city/state codes covered in ink, or whiting-out,
pushing, nubby erasering a place
to rubbery dust.

We edit, save, the record
in these young machines
we're all in, easily selectable,
highlighted, backspaced gone.

And like door knobs, thumb tacks, a box
of unburnt Nag Champa sticks in a kitchen
junk drawer we lord over, consider
what particulars we'll be able to use, later.

I update addresses, document
the wheres of stones, urns tipped in wind.
I try to rub erosions, words on graves
in Grand Gorge, whose oregano so strong
       in September.

Returning

If I were to jump this fence, shoes leading a slide
    down a canyon's shoulder, those trees at
    the bottom would catch me, excoriate
    me, and I'd deserve it.

I wasted the last four years, ignoring useful
    parts of the carrots. Drawing shades in
    midday. How long do facts about video
    games take to erase from the human
    brain? Bees escape plants without
    flowers.

Vegetable stems become soil, you can see
    through clouds built from fruit flies.
    Over a course of, say, seven thousand
    years, a stone can complete a simper.

An incredibly mysterious current event: a garage
    door is wide open, waiting for anything.

The first edition of this chapbook was originally released as a digitial edition on a small press that abruptly shut its doors in late 2017.

www.ingramcontent.com/pod-product-compliance
Lightning Source LLC
Chambersburg PA
CBHW021454080526
44588CB00009B/842